Georgia 'O' Keeffe

*She saw the world
in a flower*

Written by
Gabrielle Balkan

Illustrated by
Josy Bloggs

Georgia O'Keeffe was born on November 15, 1887, in a small town in Wisconsin. She was the second child of Francis and Ida.

Georgia's parents had grown up as neighbors, living on nearby farms. They were both third-generation immigrants. Francis's family came from Ireland and Ida's from Hungary. They were both hard workers. Everyone who lived on a farm had to be.

Georgia inherited her father's silliness and sense of adventure and shared his love of travel. "When he wanted to see the country, he just got up and went," she once said. Later in life, this is exactly what Georgia did, too.

Do you like to travel?
Where would you go and what
would you like to see?
Draw a scene from your dream vacation.

From her mother, Georgia learned to be focused,
determined, and practical. Ida was an excellent
role model. Ida and Francis had five more children
after Georgia. They were a happy family.

Georgia says her first memory was
of lying on a quilt, surrounded by
the bright light of the sun.

She was just nine months old at the time—far too young to
have any memories, said her mother. But Georgia insisted she
could remember. And when Georgia described the vivid colors
of the patchwork quilt and the details of her aunt Winnie's
dress, her mother remembered these details, too.

In another early memory, Georgia recalled the soft dirt and wooden wheels of a horse-drawn buggy. This was the vehicle that took Georgia and her sisters to town for art lessons.

What is your first memory?

Can you sketch it?

All of Georgia's early memories are filled with color.

For the first 15 years of her life, Georgia saw the same thing when she woke up and flung open the door: wheat fields, wheat fields, and more wheat fields. Miles of golden-brown feathery tips blew in the breeze, all topped by an enormous sky.

Scanning the wide horizon, Georgia would have seen the narrow road that connected their dairy farm to downtown Sun Prairie three miles away, windmills, and maybe a blackbird or two.

Georgia thought the wheat fields were beautiful. To her, they were like snow, only yellow. They transformed the landscape in spring, just as snow does in winter.

What colors do you see when you look out the window? Try painting your surroundings using just those colors.

Georgia and her sisters had two dresses each—one to wear while the other was being washed. The dresses were handmade by the girls themselves. Georgia would often see them dancing as they dried in the breeze.

After school, the sisters tended the family's vegetable patch while the brothers helped their father in the animal barn. Then they took turns on swings behind the house and played hide-and-seek in the haylofts. Sometimes Georgia would invent new games for them to play.

After dinner, the family crowded into the living room. Ida played the piano and sang. The children played dominoes or checkers. Then they would beg their mother to read aloud. Georgia loved adventure stories most of all. She especially liked to hear tales about a wilderness guide whose escapades led him across the United States, into landscapes he had never heard of.

Do you have a favorite story? Draw a picture to go with it!

But often, Georgia played alone.
One of her favorite pastimes was creating stories with a dollhouse she had made. She would carry it out to the middle of a field and play for hours by herself.

Georgia was an excellent student, especially in art.
She even won a prize for her skill at drawing.
But creating art wasn't always easy.

When she was 13, Georgia's art teacher thought her drawing
of a baby's hand was too small and too dark. Georgia was
embarrassed. She vowed to make her next drawings larger
and lighter than anyone else's. She didn't know it at the time,
but this decision would one day shake up the art world.

The next year, another teacher brought a plant into the classroom.

The teacher encouraged the students to look closely at the strange coloring and details. It was a plant Georgia had seen before but had never really examined. She was intrigued.

Look closely at a plant. What do you see? Try drawing the details.

From this moment on, Georgia found new ways to look at parts of nature that are sometimes overlooked.

Georgia wanted to be an artist, but that wasn't easy. In the early 1900s, many people expected women to teach art but not exhibit art in a museum. Georgia did teach for a time—she was a wonderful teacher, kind to her students and gifted at supporting their ideas. But teaching did not pay well.

When she could afford it, Georgia took art classes. Her classmates were fascinated by her. She dressed and acted so differently from them!

Georgia tried working in advertising. Her job was to make intricate drawings of lace. But looking closely at the lace hurt her eyes. She was relieved when that job ended.

Everything changed when Georgia went to the University of Virginia and studied with an art teacher named Arthur Dow. Georgia had been taught that an artist should faithfully copy the world around them. Arthur told her that an artist could interpret and see the world however they wanted!

This idea was revolutionary to Georgia.

Georgia was clearly talented. She could draw a windmill that looked just like the one on her family's farm. She could draw lace so beautiful that it could make someone want to buy it. But she had not yet drawn the way she wanted to draw.

She began to experiment with charcoal. Instead of drawing realistic buildings and portraits, Georgia tried something new— she used abstract shapes and sweeping lines to share a feeling.

At first glance, it might not be easy to recognize the subjects of these drawings. Yet within each one is a hint of something from nature: the graceful stalk of a plant, the curving roll of a landscape.

Experiment with charcoal and big pieces of paper. Use *abstract shapes and lines* to represent what you can see.

This was Georgia expressing herself. This was Georgia throwing off the constraints of her training.

As well as painting and drawing, Georgia loved to write letters. She wrote letters upon letters to her friends. She sometimes sent them batches of her artwork, too.

In January 1916, Georgia sent some charcoal drawings to her friend Anita Pulitzer in New York City.

Anita had seen Georgia's work before, but this new style truly astonished her. "I tell you I felt them!" she wrote back in a letter full of encouragement.

In turn, Anita shared the drawings with her friend Alfred Stieglitz. Alfred was a famous photographer who owned a famous art gallery. He used his gallery to wow the city with new talent.

Alfred was impressed by Georgia's charcoals. He decided to exhibit some of them at his gallery. Unfortunately, he did not ask Georgia's permission first!

When Georgia heard about it, she was furious. She told Alfred to remove her work from his walls.

In the end, Georgia's charcoals stayed on the walls. The show was a success, and against all odds, Georgia and Alfred became friends. From several states apart, they started sending letters, ideas, and sketches to each other. In 1918, Georgia moved to New York City, and in 1924, the two artists married.

Art was their whole world.

Alfred took photo after photo of Georgia and showed them at his famous gallery. Soon, these photos and Georgia's artwork grabbed the attention of everyone in the art world.

New York City hummed with inspiration for Georgia.
She painted the East River as she saw it from their
30th floor apartment. She painted the Brooklyn Bridge
as seen by day and towering skyscrapers as seen at
night. And she painted them all in her own unique way.

Try painting a **city scene**
at **day** *and by* **night**.
What changes did you make?

New York City was noisy, busy, and full of steel and concrete. People were everywhere she looked. Even so, Georgia found a way to connect with nature and find the solitude she so enjoyed.

Flowers in Bloom

Georgia took great pleasure in walking the city streets and made many visits to colorful flower shops. It sometimes seemed as if the rest of the city was too busy to notice the flowers. Georgia wanted to make them notice. She painted as if her paintbrush was a magnifying glass.

No one had ever painted flowers the way Georgia did.

Superb FLORISTS

Flowers in Bloom

Do you like the city or the countryside? Try zooming in on a small detail and drawing it really large!

Georgia and Alfred spent their summers and autumns
in Lake George, a small town far outside of New York
City. Finally, Georgia could garden again. She grew
corn and studied the dewdrops that ran down the
tall stalks in the morning. She painted the sturdy
green leaves, magnifying each tiny detail.

Although Georgia built herself an art studio, she often took her huge canvases outside. She liked to be as close to her subject as possible. And her subject was usually the natural world around her. When a storm came in, she watched and painted its dark gray clouds and the bright lightning forks over the waters of the lake.

Look up at the sky.
Try painting the weather.

Georgia usually painted things she found, from flowers to shells. She also painted things that can't be seen, like music. Georgia and her sisters learned to read and play music at an early age. So early, in fact, that Georgia couldn't remember a time when she couldn't read music. The violin was her favorite instrument.

Georgia challenged herself to represent music in her painting, just as she did with feelings. She experimented by using colors and shapes to show the rhythms and harmonies she heard.

Only rarely did Georgia paint people. When she did, she returned to the same subject over and over again, as she did when painting buildings, mountains, and flowers. The person she painted most was Beauford Delaney. Like Georgia, Beauford was a painter who used vibrant colors. She met him through the artists who gathered at Alfred's gallery.

In 1929, aged 41, Georgia embarked on an adventure. She was about to discover the place that would become her home forever.

A friend had invited Georgia to visit, promising space to paint, creative artists for company, and plenty of horizon to gaze at. Georgia traveled for days, from the steel buildings of New York City, through the wheat fields of her childhood, and finally arrived in the high desert of Taos, New Mexico.

Right away, the West welcomed her in a way that no other place ever had. Her eyes couldn't get enough of the crisp sky and the smooth, warm surface of the adobe homes—clay and mud buildings with flat roofs built for staying cool in the heat.

Out west, Georgia felt at home.
She invited friends and other artists to visit.
She even learned to drive, spending long days
with a friend in an old beat-up car.

For several years, Georgia divided her time between New York, where she could be with the person she loved, and New Mexico, the landscape she loved. But once Alfred died, there was only one place for Georgia: Abiquiú, New Mexico.

When Georgia walked in the desert, she collected animal bones—the skull of a cow, the pelvis and horns of a goat, a spine lying on the sand. Georgia examined the bones from every angle and looked at the sky through their small holes. And then—of course—she painted them.

What objects can you find if you go for a walk near where you live? Try drawing one floating in the sky.

She painted the bones as no one ever had:
large, oversized, as if they were the most
beautiful things in the world.

Georgia wanted to travel farther into the desert heat and work
for longer hours. To do this, she tore the seats out of her old
Ford Model A car and turned it into a traveling studio.
Now she had the independence she craved.

Georgia usually did things on her own terms, so it might have been a surprise even to her when she agreed to paint what a company asked her to.

A pineapple company in Hawaii begged Georgia to come and paint their pineapple fields. They promised her an all-expenses-paid trip. Georgia said she wasn't interested unless they let her paint in whatever way she liked. So they did. And so she went.

She hopped aboard a train, crossed the country, and boarded a boat. The trip was 5,000 miles long and took her nine days.

When she arrived, Georgia was captivated by the beautiful landscape.

At first, Georgia didn't paint what the pineapple company had hoped for—an actual pineapple. That's because they wouldn't allow her to visit the fields. It wasn't appropriate for a woman to be there with the workers, they said. So instead, Georgia toured the island, ate raw fish for the first time, and painted the black lava mountains and the lush green plants. It was all so different from her home in New Mexico.

It wasn't until she returned home that she finally painted a pineapple!

Georgia kept traveling—even into her seventies! She was always seeking adventure and finding new things to see and draw.

She took trips to Mexico, South America, Europe, India, and China. But these trips were not by train, like when she went to New Mexico, or by steamboat, as on her trip to Hawaii. Instead, Georgia traveled by plane. Flying high above the earth, she was able to admire the land below from a brand-new perspective.

Have you been on an airplane or up a tall building? Try drawing from a bird's-eye view.

Her last paintings would be of the clouds as she saw them from the airplane window. She wanted these canvases to be larger than ever before. She made them taller than she was!

She made the paintings so big, they wouldn't fit in her studio, so she had to work in a garage. Some of the canvases broke the wooden frames they were stretched on. She had to work morning to night just to cover them with paint. Some might have said that a painting this size was ridiculous, but she wanted to try.

Georgia spent her last days as she had spent her entire life—living life her way. She took long walks, gardened, cooked, read, and wrote letters. She worked hard. A favorite spot was the roof of her adobe home, where she climbed to watch the stars and sometimes sleep. She never stopped trying new things. She wrote a book, took up pottery, and made new friends. And she kept making art, even after her sight began to fail.

Before she died, Georgia asked that her ashes be spread across Pedernal, the flat mesa she loved to paint. Her home and garden are now a museum.

Georgia's paintings were loved by many, but above all, she painted for herself.

Which of Georgia's paintings *most inspire you?*

Timeline of key artworks

Georgia O'Keeffe's independent personality comes through in her art. Instead of being tied to tradition, she drew what and how she wanted. These pieces, all in the collection of The Metropolitan Museum of Art, show Georgia developing her unique style.

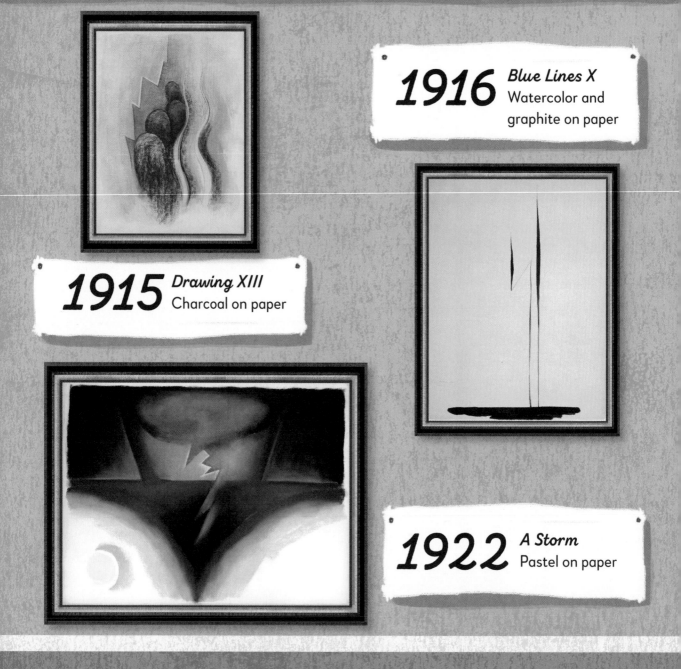

1916 *Blue Lines X*
Watercolor and graphite on paper

1915 *Drawing XIII*
Charcoal on paper

1922 *A Storm*
Pastel on paper

1925 Grey Tree, Lake George
Oil on canvas

1924 Corn, Dark, No. 1
Oil on wood fiberboard

"My painting is what I have to give back to the world *for* **what the** world **gives to me."**

–Georgia O'Keeffe, 1940

1926 Black Iris
Oil on canvas

Timeline continued:

> "It takes **more than talent.** It takes a kind of nerve ... A kind of nerve, and a lot of hard, hard work."
>
> –Georgia O'Keeffe, c. 1977

1928 East River from the Shelton Hotel
Oil on canvas

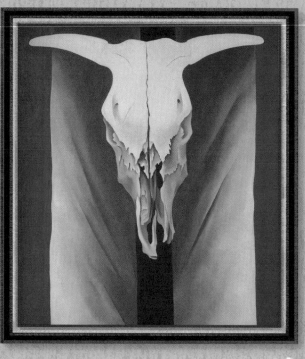

1930 Near Abiquiu, New Mexico
Oil on canvas

1931 Cow's Skull: Red, White, and Blue
Oil on canvas

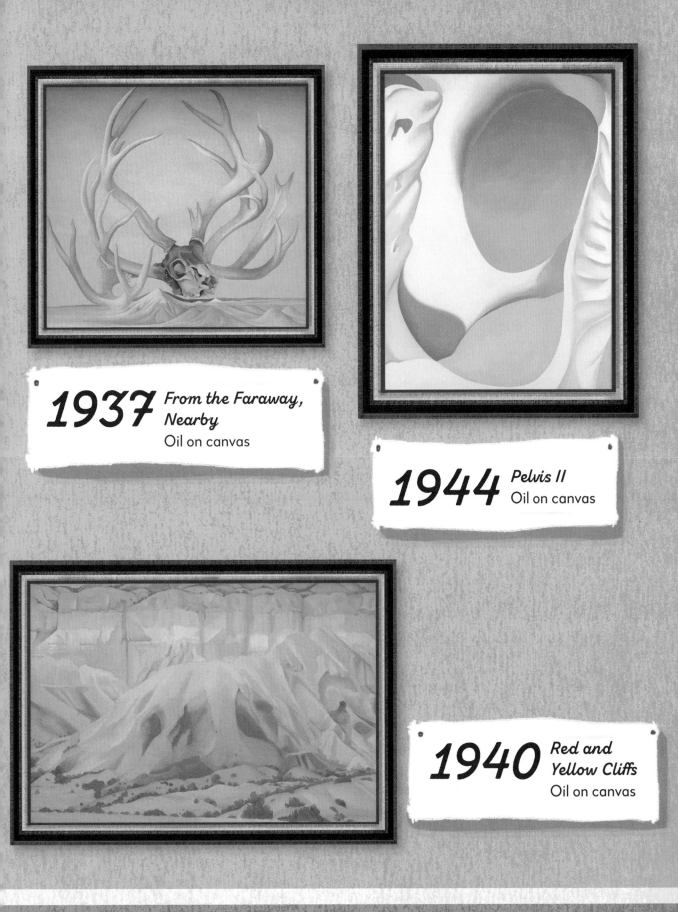

1937 From the Faraway,
Nearby
Oil on canvas

1944 Pelvis II
Oil on canvas

1940 Red and
Yellow Cliffs
Oil on canvas

Make them notice

When Georgia O'Keeffe started painting more realistic flowers, her approach was uniquely Georgia. She focused on just the blossom of a flower and enlarged the flower's smallest feature to a monumental size. Perhaps if she could surprise people with these extra-large details, they might slow down, rush less, and spend more time observing. She also used the same approach when looking at leaves, and corn, and bones in the desert.

"Nobody sees a flower really; it is so small. We haven't time, and to see takes time—like to have a friend takes time."

–Georgia O'Keeffe, 1939

Black Iris,
1926, oil on canvas

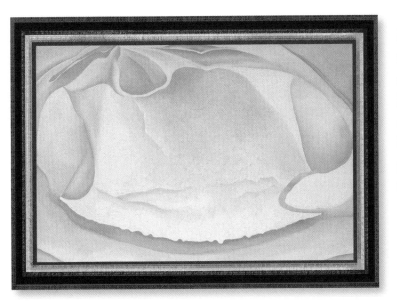

Clam Shell, 1930, oil on canvas

Now it's your turn: For this project, focus on one small part of a plant or flower and enlarge it to an unexpected size. Use pens, pencils, pastels, paints, or any medium you like.

Look for shapes *and lines that you* might *not notice at a distance.*

Corn, Dark, No. 1, 1924, oil on wood fiberboard

Instead of drawing the entire object, focus in on just one element. Crop off part of what you are studying to highlight its unexpected shapes.

Pelvis II, 1944, oil on canvas

What do you see when you look really close? Make use of a magnifying glass if you have one—or use the zoom function on a phone's camera!

Art in motion: capture a moment in time

Not everything in nature stands still long enough for an artist to study each tiny detail. Georgia challenged herself to capture something as temporary as weather, allowing her to revisit a brief moment in time.

In this painting, Georgia shares her impression of a storm. Lightning flashes across the canvas with angular red and yellow lines. These sharp edges stand out from the smudgy dark skies, clouds, and water that make up most of the picture—just like an electric bolt disturbing the night sky.

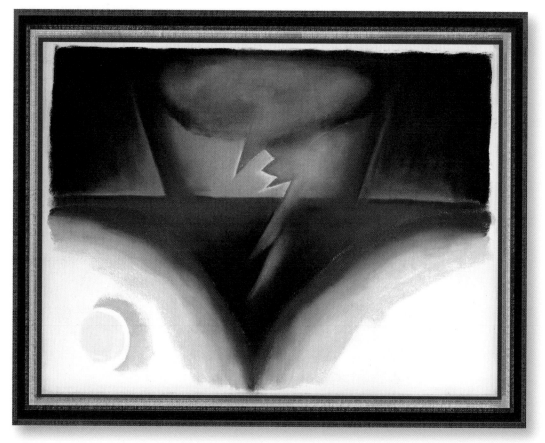

A Storm, 1922, **pastel on paper**

When the wind is blowing, look at the lines and angles that are created by moving plants, signs, or even a flyaway object!

On a rainy day, look for interesting colors reflected in puddles, or patterns in the raindrops on the window.

Try this yourself!

If it is sunny, study the shape of shadows before they change with the moving light.

Now you try: For this project, try to capture something as changeable as the weather. If you can, work outside—in the garden, the park, the beach, or anywhere that inspires you!

Glossary

abstract art *(noun)*
An art style that uses shapes, lines, and colors to represent real things. This method of interpreting the world in art form is different than **realistic art.**

canvas *(noun)*
Traditionally, an artist's canvas is made by stretching material like cotton or linen over a frame of wood, but any **medium**, such as a t-shirt or a piece of bark, can also be turned into a canvas.

charcoal *(noun)*
A black, crumbly material used as a drawing **medium**, similar to a thick pencil. Charcoal is often used for sketching an image before adding paint, but can be used on its own.

complementary colors *(noun)*
Two colors that look vibrant, as opposed to dull, next to one another. Complementary colors are created when you place one primary color with the secondary color made from the remaining two primary colors. For instance, the primary color yellow is a complementary color to the secondary color purple. They are opposite each other on the color wheel.

composition (*noun*)

How images are organized on an artwork.
Artists use patterns, contrast, and other visual
tools to develop a certain composition.

medium (*noun*)

Refers to what an artist is drawing with and what they
are drawing on. Different types of medium include:
all sorts of paint (such as oil or watercolor), drawing
material (such as **charcoal**, pastel, or pencil),
and **canvas** (such as wood or paper).

modernism/modern art (*noun*)

Describing art that was created from approximately
the 1860s through the 1970s. Modern artists
experimented with materials, techniques, and imagery
to represent emotion and ideas. This approach
is different than that of **realistic art**.

realism/realistic art (*noun*)

Describing art that was created to show the world as it
might appear in real life. The resulting image is "true" to
life, without any exaggeration. This approach has been
used during many different periods in time and is one
way of interpreting the world, as **abstract art** is another.

About the author

Gabrielle Balkan writes about animals, geography, and anything else she wants to learn more about. When she was a high-school student in Indianapolis, Indiana, Gabrielle dressed up as Georgia O'Keeffe and pretended a banana was one of the desert bones that Georgia painted. Gabrielle now lives in New York and, with her twin fifth graders, likes to draw pictures of their guinea pigs, find geocaches, and write postcards to help increase voter turnout. Gabrielle is grateful to all of those who have written about inspiring artists, including Roxana Robinson, the author of *Georgia O'Keeffe: A Life.*

About the artist

Based in Yorkshire, UK, Josy Bloggs began her initial career as a graphic designer. After graduating from the University of Huddersfield with an MA in Spatial Design, she went on to work as an interior designer for commercial clients. Josy loves working with layout and color to create impactful illustration and enjoys combining illustration with type and font selection to create a balance between text and image. When she is not creating, she is busy looking after her horse, dog, and two cats.

Author's note/further reading

It's a tricky thing to try and capture all 98 years of someone's life into just a handful of pages. Luckily, there are many books about Georgia O'Keeffe, and by reading some—or all!—of them, you can get a better idea about the person and artist she was. And hopefully be inspired to create your own art.

Here are some resources you may enjoy:

Georgia Rises: A Day in the Life of Georgia O'Keeffe
by Kathryn Lasky and Ora Eitan

My Name is Georgia: A Portrait by Jeanette Winter

Georgia in Hawaii: When Georgia O'Keeffe Painted What She Pleased
by Amy Novesky and Yuyi Morales

We Are Artists: Women Who Made Their Mark on the World by Kari Herbert

Senior Editor Emma Grange
Senior Designer Anna Formanek
Project Editor Beth Davies
Editor Julia March
Designer Zoë Tucker
Picture Researchers Martin Copeland,
Sumedha Chopra, and Sumita Khatwani
Production Editor Siu Yin Chan
Senior Production Controller Lloyd Robertson
Managing Editor Paula Regan
Managing Art Editor Jo Connor
Publishing Director Mark Searle

First American Edition, 2021
Published in the United States by DK Publishing
1450 Broadway, Suite 801, New York, NY 10018

Page design copyright © 2021 Dorling Kindersley Limited
DK, a Division of Penguin Random House LLC
21 22 23 24 25 10 9 8 7 6 5 4 3 2
003–322786–Aug/2021

The Metropolitan
Museum of Art
New York

© The Metropolitan Museum of Art

A catalog record for this book
is available from the Library of Congress.
ISBN 978-0-7440-3367-0

DK books are available at special discounts when purchased in bulk for sales
promotions, premiums, fund-raising, or educational use. For details, contact:
DK Publishing Special Markets,
1450 Broadway, Suite 801, New York, NY 10018
SpecialSales@dk.com

Printed and bound in China

Acknowledgments
DK would like to thank Randall Griffey, Lisa Silverman Meyers, Laura
Barth, Leanne Graeff, Emily Blumenthal, and Morgan Pearce at The Met;
Hilary Becker; Julie Ferris and Lisa Lanzarini; Kayla Dugger;
and Gabrielle Balkan and Josy Bloggs.

Author's dedication: To my very own Georgia Grey,
an artist from the get go.

For the curious

www.dk.com
www.metmuseum.org